# The Morgan

Rachel Damon Criscione

The Rosen Publishing Group's

**PowerKids Press**™

New York

*To my son Nicholas Criscione.*
*A special thanks to Kathy Furr of The National Museum of the Morgan Horse*
*in Shelburne, Vermont.*

Published in 2007 by The Rosen Publishing Group, Inc.
29 East 21st Street, New York, NY 10010

First Edition

Editors: Melissa Acevedo and Amelie von Zumbusch
Book Design: Ginny Chu

Photo Credits: Cover, title page, pp. 4, 14 © Bob Langrish/Animals Animals; p. 7 Photograph Collection of the National Museum of the Morgan Horse, Shelburne, Vermont; p. 8 © Bob Krist/Corbis; p. 11 The Sherman Black Hawk image from the Photograph Collection of the National Museum of the Morgan Horse, Shelburne, Vermont; p. 12 © Kevin R. Morris/Corbis; p. 15 Jerry Cooke/Animals Animals; p. 16 © AMHA; p. 19 Margot Conte/Animals Animals; p. 20 photo and pedigree courtesy of denlorephoto.com.

Library of Congress Cataloging-in-Publication Data

Criscione, Rachel Damon.
  The Morgan / Rachel Damon Criscione.
      p. cm. — (The Library of horses)
  Includes bibliographical references and index.
  ISBN 1-4042-3451-9 (lib. bdg.)
  1. Morgan horse—Juvenile literature.  I. Title.
  SF293.M8C75 2007
  636.1'77—dc22
                                    2005028073

Manufactured in the United States of America

# Table of Contents

All Morgans, including the horse to the right, are related to a horse called Figure. Figure was born in Massachusetts in the late 1700s. Today Morgan horses live in all 50 U.S. states and more than 20 other countries.

# The Morgan

In 1789, a horse named Figure was born in New England. In time Figure became the **foundation sire** for an entire **breed** of horses. This breed, the Morgan, became so popular that it was named the official horse of the state of Vermont. It is the only breed of horse named after a person.

Justin Morgan, after whom Morgans were named, was the farmer who owned the small horse called Figure. He **bred** Figure with other horses and soon Figure's **offspring** became popular in northern New England. The Morgans, as they became known, had Figure's strength and were well suited to climbing steep hills. The Morgan soon became one of the most important breeds in America.

# Justin Morgan and Figure

Justin Morgan was a teacher and farmer. In the 1780s, Morgan was given a horse that he named Figure. Figure was a small, bay horse. Bay horses have reddish brown coats and black manes and tails. Morgan brought Figure along with him when his family moved from Springfield, Massachusetts, to Randolph, Vermont.

Once the Morgans were in their new home, they put Figure to work clearing trees from fields and pulling wagons. Soon Morgan's horse, as Figure was also known, proved that what he lacked in size he made up for in strength. In time Figure won a log-pulling event, carried President James Monroe in a parade, and outran many horses. Figure became a very well known horse.

JUSTIN MORGAN

Figure, shown here, was the father of many horses. Some of his most well known children were called Sherman Morgan, Woodbury Morgan, and Bulrush Morgan. One of his grandsons was named Black Hawk.

The farmers of northern New England needed strong horses to work on their hilly farms. The farm shown here is near Woodstock, Vermont.

# Hardworking Horses

Soon the farmers in Randolph, Vermont, asked Justin Morgan to breed Figure with their horses. Figure quickly became very popular among horse breeders. This is because Figure's offspring would receive the horse's many talents and strengths. Many of the farmers in the area wanted Morgans, because these horses are well suited to working on the steep hills of northern New England. This made Figure's offspring useful to the farmers.

After Justin Morgan died in 1798, Figure was passed from owner to owner. He spent the remainder of his life working in Vermont and New Hampshire. Figure worked long and hard until he died in 1821.

# Dependable Transportation

As the population of the United States grew in the 1800s, so did the need for horses. At this time some Morgans continued to work on farms as Figure had. Other Morgans began to be used for **transportation**. Big cities, like New York, Boston, and Chicago, brought Morgans from New England farms to use for public transportation. By 1870, nearly all the horses used to pull streetcars and **carriages** in big cities were Morgans. These dependable horses also carried mail and cleared land so roads and cities could be built.

In the early 1900s, cars began taking the place of horses for transportation. Farmers also started using machines called tractors to do farmwork instead of using horses. The number of Morgans in America began to go down.

Morgans drew many kinds of carriages in the 1800s. This horse is drawing a sulky. A sulky is a small cart with two wheels and a single seat. Sulkies are often used for racing.

This Morgan is taking part in a horse show at the Kentucky Horse Park in Lexington, Kentucky.

# A Multipurpose Horse

As heavy machinery began to be used more commonly in the twentieth century, horses were no longer needed to pull streetcars or to work on farms. However, many people found that although they no longer needed horses, they still enjoyed owning them. Morgans soon were ridden for pleasure rather than work. Today the multipurpose Morgan is used mostly for exercise and fun.

Morgans take part in all kinds of sporting and driving events. These horses are usually entered in English- and Western-style riding events, horse shows, and trail rides. Some Morgans even train for **dressage**. Dressage is a type of riding that requires small, controlled movements. It looks almost like dancing!

# Small but Strong!

A Morgan's body is round and firm. Morgans are known for their bright **expressive** eyes, strong legs, broad chest, and short back. Morgans come in many colors, including black, brown, and

gray. They commonly have a few small white markings below the knee. Morgans are known for their strength, gentle nature, and ability to finish jobs quickly.

Morgans are average sized. They stand between 14 and 15 hands (1.4–1.5 m) tall. Hands are a kind of measurement that is equal to 4 inches (10 cm). Horses all over the world are measured in hands. Morgans are measured from the ground to their withers, which is the dent between their shoulder bones.

Morgans are known for their small ears and their wide heads.

The Morgan shown here is named Canequin's Film Star. Morgans, such as Canequin's Film Star, are gentle and calm horses.

# Gentle Creatures

Morgans are valued around the world for their strength, beauty, and speed. They are friendly, smart, and gentle enough for both beginners and advanced riders to use them.

Some Morgans are used as **therapeutic riding** horses. These horses take part in events for children and adults with special needs. People who are blind, in wheelchairs, or ill sometimes ride therapeutic riding horses. The Morgans that are used are mostly older horses who have been trained to work with people who may need special attention. Trainers work with both the horses and the riders. The rider must learn to trust the horse. In turn the horse learns not to be scared by unexpected movements.

# Caring for a Morgan

To raise such smart, gentle creatures, the owners of Morgans need to supply them with food, housing, water, and exercise. A Morgan's meal changes depending on the time of year, its age, and the amount of work it does. In the summer Morgans eat mostly grass. When the ground is bare in the winter, the horse eats green hay and grain with **vitamins** mixed in.

As all horses do, Morgans make their feelings known through tail movements. When their tail is held high, it means they are happy. A hanging tail means the horse is sad, afraid, or tired. If its tail is swishing back and forth, a horse may be angry. This is just one way Morgans let people know how they are feeling.

Horses roll in the grass to keep their coat healthy. They get rid of extra hair from their coat when they roll. Even if a horse gets dusty when it rolls, the dust keeps the horse safe from bugs and the sun.

# AMERICAN MORGAN HORSE REGISTER

REGISTRATION　　　CERTIFICATE

№ 122880

This Certifies that the Morgan　　STALLION

Named　DENLORE'S DESERT STORM

Foaled　April 17, 1991　　Color BROWN

Bred by　　　　0849422
DENNIS & MARCELLA TATRO
HARTFORD, VERMONT

Marked　SMALL SNIP.

THE GLITTER MERCHANT
107195

TUG HILL COMMANDO
85508

WILLY'S WHISPER
080599

DENLORE'S DESERT STORM 122880

THANKYOU DEARLY
079567

EQUINOX MARAUDER
64903

PARAMOUNT'S MADONNA
023489

WASEEKA'S IN COMMAND
16031

FIDDLER'S MAJESTA
071900

TREBLE'S WILLY WILD
67948

BREN BERN EUNIDOR
019585

GREEN MEADS MARAUDER
11903

EQUINOX QUIET LEA
022574

PARAMOUNT AMBASSADOR
13224

PARAMOUNT'S HI-DONNA
016984

WASEEKA'S NOCTURNE 11181
MILLER'S ADEL 09177
KADENVALE DON 12346
FIDDLER'S CAMEO 020256
WINDY HILL WILLIE 20865
JUNEHILL FASCINATION 020452
WINDCREST WINFIELD 12098
STOCKBRIDGE PENNY 012997
UPWEY BEN DON 8843
ABBINGTON OF SHADY LAWN
07389
BALD MT EBONY KNIGHT 12373
GLADGAY'S LADY LEA 013268
UPWEY BEN DON 8843
BETTY ROSS 05555
ORCLAND DONDARLING 12261
PARAMOUNT'S BARONESS 011473

is registered in the American Morgan Horse Register

Given under my hand and seal, at New York, on

July 07, 1993

THE AMERICAN MORGAN HORSE ASSOCIATION, INC.

Executive Director

Record Owner　　　1063221
DENNIS L & LAURA A TATRO
HARTFORD, VERMONT

This is a pedigree of Denlore's Desert Storm, a Morgan. Pedigrees trace the history and bloodlines of an individual horse. The picture above shows Denlore's Desert Storm.

# The American Morgan Horse Association

The Morgan Horse Club started at a fair in White River Junction, Vermont, in 1909. At this fair people showed their Morgans and decided to form a club in honor of these animals. In 1971, the club's name became the American Morgan Horse Association (AMHA). The group has members in more than 20 countries around the world. Its purpose is to keep records and provide histories of Morgans for their owners.

AMHA sets down requirements for a horse to be considered a Morgan. One requirement is that both of a horse's parents must be Morgans. Many Morgan events also require owners to prove their horses are pure Morgans.

# Congress Helps the Morgan

By the early 1900s, the number of Morgans in the United States began to go down. Even though Morgans were still valued for their strength and beauty, people wanted taller and faster horses. People began breeding Morgans with horses of other breeds. Even though their offspring were quicker and taller, they were no longer pure Morgans.

In 1905, the U.S. Congress voted to create a farm to keep the Morgan alive. This farm would also raise horses for the U.S. **cavalry**. In 1907, the United States Morgan Horse Farm was founded in Weybridge, Vermont. After the cavalry was done away with in 1951, the United States Department of Agriculture gave the farm to the University of Vermont. The university still runs the farm today.

# Glossary

bred (BRED)  Brought a male and a female animal together so they will have babies.

breed (BREED)  A group of animals that look alike and have the same relatives.

carriages (KAR-ij-ez)  Wheeled objects used to carry people or things.

cavalry (KA-vul-ree)  The part of an army that rides and fights on horseback.

dressage (dreh-SAZH)  A French term that means "training." The horse and rider do ballet-type movements that show off the horse's balancing skills, if it is bendable, and if it obeys.

expressive (ek-SPREH-siv)  Full of meaning and feeling.

foundation sire (fown-DAY-shun SY-er)  The founding father of a breed of animals.

offspring (OF-spring)  The product of two parents brought together to make babies.

therapeutic riding (ther-uh-PYOO-tik RY-ding)  A method of riding for people with special needs that aims to heal or help them.

transportation (tranz-per-TAY-shun)  A way of traveling from one place to another.

vitamins (VY-tuh-minz)  Nutrients that help the body fight illness and grow strong.

# Index

# Web Sites

Due to the changing nature of Internet links, PowerKids Press has developed an online list of Web sites related to the subject of this book. This site is updated regularly. Please use this link to access the list:

www.powerkidslinks.com/horse/morgan/